We're the Drug

A Collection of Poetry

By

Justin Everett Foyil

To Christine,
Keep writing your ass off!
And don't break ya neck
lookin for ya mum!

Your Pal,

We're the Drug
All contents © 2016 by Justin Everett Foyil
All Right Reserved.

Published by: Coyote Blood Press.
Paradisiac Publishing.

No part of this book may be reproduced
without expressed written permission of the author
or the publisher, except for brief quotes for review purposes.

Poetic Contributing Editor/American
Ryan Buynak
www.coyoteblood.blogspot.com

Author Contact:
www.werethedrug.com
www.facebook.com/werethedrug

Awesome Cover Art by: Paige Arnett

Cover Designed by: C.J. Boger

ISBN-13: 978-1535318914
ISBN-10: 1535318910

To care

Is to love

And to feel

Is a drug

In you.

Dedicated
To artists everywhere
Bleeding creation without fear,
And to the best writer I know...

Ryan Buynak
a.k.a.
Coyote Blood.

The more you learn about me…

the less you know about me.

Wearable Ink

Don't have to explain my art to you
if your suit doesn't fit the mold,
or dress; depending the occasion.

That's what your mind is for,
your answer.

Casual isn't allowed here,
so dress yourself…

(In caution).

Talk Hard

I'm not afraid
to bring up the unspoken,
looking for twists and turns with words
to sway the emotion you've held
deep inside.

Feed off me,
off my words,
allow yourself to get off…
as I am with you
in conversation.

Experience
is value taken notice of,
enabling you to question and rise
and finally feel what it means
to be alive.

Allowing you to see
that there is more out there.

More to talk about, more to breathe for,
more to love than them,
more to love…

Than yourself.

Arson

Listen
to our conviction through silence,
we hear bells
ringing the atmosphere to move us,
to mesh our thoughts,
to make us believe
in anything worth fighting for!

Anything of substance,
anything worth a fuck!

Our idea of placement for artistic minds,
no longer held down by triggers
firing visions of normal our way.
No longer wearing their failed attempts
to lead us where we don't belong.

Fight!
Every soul named Distraction.
Armed with passion,
we are more than people.

Together,
we are emotion.
Together,
we are change.

Forever bleeding words,
our movement for difference.
We're the Drug!

An idea possessed,
holding our souls with steady hands
and never letting go
until we're all creating free!

Anti-Heroes

Defiant
We live lives
Fading corners
Over forty-five
Floating limitless
Over law-abiding skies
Under our rules
Inside style
Holding art
Drifting
Never falling
Apart.

Spark

We are all just words
with revisions of words,
a feeling, undefined.

Just as your love story,
your prime.

Now dive into reason:
you're the gas, fueling these words.
(My propane habit).

Discrete with sensitivity
while seeping through bars,
into this heart.

Now enlightened
from your illumination,
wearing glasses of you
because my eyes only see so far…

And now open, to the world.

Perfect Stranger

Can we get an appraisal
for how much we exist?

You are the princess of always,
so let's celebrate our chemistry.

Tell me you love me,
then breathe with me.

Share your tendencies
to make me feel alive again,
through feeling.

Kiss me to want me,
then bleach your past.

(Mine is darker than white can save).

So save me,
then take me,
past places words are allowed.

Who we are
is not their concern,
and who we are…

(They will never learn).

We belong here together
while our song remains the same,
so believe it, then dream it, that place

Where our hearts beat for sound.

Guile

Voice
is overrated,
Out Loud.

We live in minds,
though strange it seems
Home.

Gasp the breath of you
already taken in before spoken,
descending the idea of you
faster than a right hand can type: y.o.u.

Captions of your monologue
now throttled back,
making room for the thoughts that matter
to finally be conveyed.

We Are

We float on air
above dreams,
transcribing words
only we can hear.

Bleeding creation, without fear.

Grinning shades of laughter
as we leave them behind,
with weapons up, heads down,
we're crossing barriered lines.

Our souls
willing to die,
to rise our voice at any cost.

Immersing everything held inside
from a lifetime,
spent lost.

Art Of Aggression

All I want
is to be affected
by something
someone
anything
with effect
flowing
creating ideas
starting movements
following no one
thinking inside
barriers of chaos
outside patience
always patient
breaking free
learning cold

Now show your face.

Rewind

Washing out water with water,
think of who you are.

Be the ramble on their tongues.
Throw inadequate judgments aside.
Be an epic poem without meaning.
Describe the face without words.
Careless, cunning, and unfair.

Feel without touch.
Learn your false truth.
Laugh you're alive.
Sleep when you're dead.

Create the uncreatable.
Leave the past behind.
Act out lucid dreams.
Be free in your playground.
Their minds.

Pretend to love.
Tear down walls.
Whisper loud.
Cry silence.

Walk above fear.
Dress for danger.
Talk without age, and kiss rage.
Pluralize lone.
Rangers.

Shake hands with heroes.
Use lethal thoughts.
Fuel the extinguished.
The lost.

Pierce superficial meaning.
Learn and forget.
Play with the weak.
Spill paper black, without ink.

Fall with style.
Hurt without pain.
Grieve with a grin.
Offend.

Damage materialism.
Make up isms.
Dress without matching, naked.
Pornism.

Dig for maps, and treasure direction.
Make up your own language.
Speak without sound.
Be profound.

Always play with their minds.

Rewind.

Extinguish Silence

Today is your day,
so take a picture to freeze your time
ever felt alive.

Someday this all will end,
so don't give up like them.

A ghost of you is no braver than the rest.

Never settle,
never blame luck,
because that's fucking life,
we all get stuck!

Crush the words without a cure!

Allow your feelings to burn
from your chest through your mind,
assuring your heart
to scream out everything inside!

Now extinguish silence, and let the flames begin!

An American Horror Story

An intriguing dance
of our own device,
an epic chance
for sacrifice.

Thoughts unknown
we forget to share,
a *Colt* gun
now summon the atmosphere.

A tower watching over
a world now clear,
with red lips,
black eye liner,
and words to bear.

Now tell me your story,
ideas I beg to fear,
from bright lights,
dark songs,
everything I need to hear.

We wrote these lines once
through minds without words,
because you could never bring it together
and speak of the love…

We deserved.

Obsession

Your joy
is my obsession,
a lesson.

Cultivating receptors
turning keys
inside a heart I've never met.

(My Static Twisted Ritual).

So violate me,
entertain the notion
that we belong.

Through fragile minds,
due to comment in time.

This Room

Inside these walls
lies my playground,
blue-lit for response.

Turning word into lyric,
and voice into song.

You'd sleep well here
camouflaged in tranquility,
forever surrounded
with arms of love.

Once lost
now found together,
as the world outside drifts away.

With our future imagined
slowly turning present,
lucid dreams become reality.

Now you're the air filling these lungs:
taking in all the love you give
exhaling the best of me…

For the rest of our days.

3:14

This is time
delayed again…

Lagging on schedule
this pen articulates silent thoughts the most.

Shit just got real!
Sounds like a candle-burning situation,
for time of night.

When writing flows sideways,
impossible is not a word.

Coming from nowhere
from nothing,
with no one, to be found.

Decorated Emergency

I write for arthritis,
the length it takes
to reach true creation.

The way *Forests* sway
and *run* with wind,
to truly show themselves.

To fill this desire,
this ticking fire
burning to create,
needed more
than humans need water,
for survival.

Without pens or keys
I. Am. Nothing.
but a blank notion of yesterday,
with nothing left to say.

Lit

I'm getting high right now
(with words).

A different kind of lit
for this pen blowing smoke
(eager to emit).

Blazing stories
shared through our minds,
exhaling our existence
(ever since its ignition).

All while this flame burns
lighting up inspiration,
forever fueling thoughts in waiting
(for the next idea to spark).

Striking Matches

These tobacco filled lungs
can slow down time
(processing you slower).

Your words
filtering smoke
(while speeding up this heart).

A forest
burning sweet with mystery,
steady addiction drawing me in
(while signaling desire).

Inhaling a scent
different from the everyday
(fragrance of normality).

Allowing you to enter
while sweeping under me
(my ghost of fog inversed).

Lift me up, now fall me apart
while wrenching this heart
(under scarlet touch).

Now possessed
(I'm finally understood).

Here's To The Puppet Show

Sorry I'm late, got held up
(at gunpoint).
Her personality
always tried to shoot me down.

That's the sound of my past
(always a dangerous trend).
So don't kiss me, unless you mean it.

Three twenty-three a.m. and thirteen seconds…
(a time remembered most).
That began my falling, over her.

Carried along with purse, was a temper
(like the forefront of a minefield).
Ready to go off at any given time.

Well I like you, but could go off you
(so I did five times before it stuck).
That's why five is still my favorite number
after all these years.

Cheers!

Lines

Aging.
Disconnect.
Stimulants.
Desire.
Words.
Withered.
Anger.
Search.
Fear.
Sex.
Judgment.
Dramatic.
Pause.
Laughter.

Cult

Misfits
rock kicks
same shoes
filled with shit.

Get ripped
tight-lipped
wordless feelings
holding whys
cross-stitched together
free inside.

Time to *Recover*
for us to *Shiiine*
three eyes
two paths
one life…

Spilling time.

Pendulum

Did I lose you
from caring too much
to hide inside?

Now I stain,
like your eyes do
with visions of us.

Instead,
all of mine are seen
holding only you.

Through flashbacks of feelings,
from a time felt before.

Behind eyes unable to lie
you said so yourself
that "we wouldn't survive."

This pool only gets deeper…

So if it's meant to be, then you'll find me.

Create To Escape

We are all souls
never having to hide,
with five senses forever feeding us
the notion to sway.

Arming emotion, undercover,
to move us back to forward,
our motion, toward feel,
spawning imagination.

That movement inside us all
toward unfamiliar,
guiding our ambition
outside inherited tradition.

Now induce mastery,
inspiring reign.
Through creation
find out where you belong.
Become the best at who you are!

Found out with time…
your perfect utensil for influence,
while drawing in their resistance.

So paint your purpose
as a portrait to touch,
portrayed behind a glass case
spot-lit for direction.

To inspire
their reasons for believing,
until they are all strong enough
to break through understanding.

Jessic

Together we think like fragrance,
sharing desirable thoughts of mystery.
Lost in search of source,
then found in each other's minds.

I love playing here,
and off your words,
off the grid of the everyday,
my new-child-game of old.

We communicate through art,
it's our own sign language.

Just another smell of familiar
while painting scenes we've shared,
reflected in each other's eyes.

Forever losing ourselves in company
with a dedication to different,
now our rehabilitation
toward making a difference.

United At Different
(For R & K)

United at different
dangerous minds collide,
adhering together now
for life.

So take me with your every day
hand in hand for this ride we believe,
mixing our chemicals with words
creating a love, unheard.

Now we begin…
the first day of our last days,
immortal as one.

Through a sound portal of fear
together we'll rise,
where there's more to be had
never to end,
sparked from this beginning's end.

You are the perfect drug
stimulating me still,
without a sound
breathing words that make my eyes close,
a feeling so hard, still undefined.

'Til death do us part
ignite the fire felt inside our chests,
then forever apart we'll always be

From the rest.

Stomach

The days I *bear*,
seem *eating* me away.

Like glass to *walls*,
inside *hunger* for art.

Digested everyday,
while *lining* my future.

Now *swallowed* in waiting,
as I *abide* with time.

Metric

I rhyme hard with words
even when they don't sound alike,
for style, unique.

Clever pieces unnoticed,
endorsed with ink.

Intricate thoughts
rhythmic without sound,
feeble in their eyes, all the same.
Those inartistic minds
(puzzled for sight).

Nonetheless,
these words forever flow on edge
framing creativity
along with their dissension,
blended together.
Making it easier on those eyes
still lost for sight
(to picture genius).

They speak, then I scream,
ideas higher than they can reach!
As this fever rises
holding their inspiration
(forever fueling my temperature!).

Through sleepless…
nights have become my days.
Spending most writing fast
to help think slow,
all while coming down with words, a cold
(this sickness I'll never shake).

Now with ink, the venom
coursing the blood in these veins.
My only ethical drug
for daily escape.

Now
come back to earth,
revising lines
while clocks tick hours for time,
just to help them comprehend,
and appreciate the creativity
fueling this gas-filled pen.

Igniting everything
that their lost souls are lacking within.

Though set in their ways with age,
and from growing up near fear of change,
I set fire to their world!
Drawing blood from their anemic hearts
(drowning in screams of blue).

Now I'm giving air
to the feelings they've tried to hide,
until they're enlightened
and sparks fly all over skies.

Now and forever,
they will feel the message I've bled,
bringing out the insides of their being
to finally start, being.

Once believed
and seen through inspired eyes glowing red,
once and for all,
finally filling their clarity for sight…

I will silence this pulse
beating words…

(Unsaid).

Posture Up

Never negate talent while it's happening,
or mistake confidence for ego.

This assured feeling I hold
while writing to you...

(Eating my *Eggo* waffle).

Thieve Me Please

Don't rhyme with me
if you can't keep up.

Don't lie with me
if you can't be up for it.

Night after night
dwelling lines of past…

Situations gathering thoughts
harder, than you feel lost.

Now rhyme again
with me in your own way.

Particularly with conviction,
or I won't understand.

So stand, and laugh hard,
and speak proud,
and sing loud!

To forgive our sound.

Ray Ray Virgil

I love
top-shelf liquor
and dancing
with *werds*
upon devils
inside blogs
outside boxes
around shapes
of usual
amused
usually
then go back
through crowds
of whiskey
to dancing.

The Stoop

This place I've never seen
always seems to create things
evolving me.

Straight from the source,
from the heart.

With written words emitting smoke,
unveiling who you are
in moments.

Within every thought your eyes portray,
no matter what scene surrounds you,
your scripted words always take me there.

The real inside you
is where I *live,* reflected.

That place
where you thrive,
endlessly filling this mind
(with ideas of a lesser kind).

October Air

Breeze your thoughts
toward open windows,
letting imagination
run free in the light.

Night
never felt this way,
sinking degrees
that inspire within.

Now enter:
fluorescent skies and time.
(When I create the most).

While ghosts
walk the earth,
flaunting that they're still alive.

Now allow me to feel the same
and believe this world is mine,
to create through its living canvas
and prove that art will never die.

Cordless

Surprised
no ring on this one
a morning
calling different
some day
back in feelings
out of February
guess we're all growing up
except me
already been to that place
out of Octobers
learning coffee
for winters
revived
writing this
caffeinated
while talking to you
and you'll never know
the line you just spoke
floored me
guess I'm still learning
still getting older
and you'll never know
what it really meant
as you laughed
at the end
like always

(Now it is).

Soundtrack

Surround me with dreams
to forward me ahead
to a time well wanted,
above all things.

To play in clouds with sound
raining steady notes below melodic skies,
drawn from this reality
written over time.

Combining words,
building books,
writing lines,
voicing songs.

Fading day after night, now seemed
just turning chapters compiled together,
never to be seen.

Jumping off pages,
waving from speakers,
crashing into ears
needing to hear…

The end to this list
of never ending albums I've saved,
some place called Patient
still undefined,
while the world awaits.

Soon ahead will come the time
sought forever in mind,
spinning records perfectly flawed,
the soundtrack of this life
to be remembered by them all.

Can You See Me In The Dark?

Visualize the time
when I believe the most,
infamous for words
while I'm eating toast.

Forever fucking with your mind,
testing its potential
while creating moments to live by.

So follow me
to the place where I can see sound,
planting melodies inside rhymes
then Starring them…

In the back of your mind.

Timeless

Time machines don't exist,
but I'll lend you mine.

(Forever held in mind).

To twist this life,
this ride,
to feel the meaning inside
these words,
this heart,
to understand the difference
between your time…

And mine.

Time

We both ended up in this place
from different paths of nowhere,
perfect strangers united
from a time well waited.

Before
we were ticking people away…
friends and lovers alike,
one second at a time.

The ones that lasted hours
we called Best,
then without choice, or voice,
still counted them away the same.

Now
as seconds turn into years,
time flows different in direction
with you still here.

So only forever
can engrave the day,
that two dark paths finally came alive
from intersecting ways.

Together
now changed,
time will never count the same.

Lost Highway

High beams
seep through ghosts of fog
as *Civil Twilight* plays background,
holding memories of you.

The ones I've stored
far too deep to speak of.

Gleams of light
now push through trees,
casting our spotlight in this town,
seen unfamiliar.

Inhaling art
through sight and sound
as this car drives slower,
gathering thoughts, through thought,
every window by shutter passed.

I can hear the world speak in this moment
saying *there's more to be had...*
breathing inspiration through the wind
for a changing path to come.

I search for a button to push
to capture this feel forever,
but for now
pictured only in mind.

Just another memory
filled with you,
stored away.

Typewriter

What would we be now
if we never wasted us?

We were rebels
without a cause,
without a cure.

Now I only hear you through walls,
playlists telling your story
hidden from us all.

This is the first time shelling out words
I know there's no turning back.

It's exhilarating
knowing these thoughts are flowing from a lost source
never to be lost again.

Feelings come out differently
when they can't be erased…

Speaking words louder than love,
like the meaning of *doorways*
where you used to stand,
forever here to stay.

We may lose our way
before we find our story,
but no one will ever stop our path.

We Are The Past

Falling stones
now become
floating feathers
Over this city
across their world
Charging
through walls
along waves
Into minds
amongst hearts
every day
Against odds.

Under Her

Spellbound for trouble
under spells
under witness
under her
always
revamping feelings
uniting mistakes
holding hearts
through earthquakes
kissing jeans
and things you used to walk in
now left behind
with rivers
turning streams
now miss me
before rivers
run blood to seas
washing away
the stain of a love
once worn
still surrounding me.

The Price Of Kissing

A feeling this deep
remains unwritten,
until felt.

Then words come pouring
from the blood of my heart
through this pen,
as I melt.

I love all the things
you do to move me,
assuring words through stares
only your eyes could prepare.

Now leveled off,
and forgot is the world
as our seams join.

Lost,
now no longer a word
with our hearts deployed.

Two Of Kind

Together
we're like each other's infatuation
grounded by reason.

A decade
over the influence,
swaying all degrees of emotion
within a commercial-breaks-time.

Ground me,
from flying cold in 120 degree weather,
feed me love then guilt
in admirable ways.

We talk in art
it's our own slang,
an understanding
with only pencils, brushes, and melodies.

(They never could).

Now try and replicate
through color who we are,
unattainable.

With precision
perfectly flawed,

We are one.

Triggered Pictures

You
on film
reeling
with emotion.

Me
a lost soldier
fighting no one
but myself.

Now
I give you my love
without my heart
still in the spotlight
unafraid.

Jet

Life took a trip today
around the world and back,
short route, long reel, and me
laughing at the feel.

Flying through joke-weather:
those cloudy times
when your emotions give in
to their surroundings.

Somehow
getting the best of you,
a place I've seen
though never belonged.

In these times
a level mind is all that's needed,
over and over, to overcome.

Because "if you stand for nothing
then you'll fall for anything,"
left only wondering
where you went wrong.

The Escapist

I wish I had a passport filled with stamps
so I could say "I've been there."

But for now I'm just gonna chug beers
until I'm good at something...

And travel in mind.

Difference

My mind is fucked up…
taking daily trips to tangent cities
using words for transportation.

"Well you asked for it,"
a brother once told me.

Through prayers for art,
and for the ability to create.
Hoping to evoke change in peoples lives,
expressing ideas differently
to make a difference.

Now I've become a victim
of my own vision,
and the difference is living with it.

Carrying around a mind
with a mind of its own,
with the results for difference…

Still waiting to be seen.

Tangent

The blonde on the television set
has now become my muse
for words.

[Pigtails optional].

Even without...
she gives me everything
to hold on to.

Her thoughts and ambition ring... of fire,
lighting a pilot light in my life.

Someone once told me that I did that for them,
since we shared the same taste
in old fashion.

Fashion,
being music clothed the right way,
and old
is what is becoming of me.

I guess that's true for both of our souls
growing up in that era.
(90s grunge movement lives!).

Maybe if I wrote the word "lives"
with a crooked *i*,
you would know I meant "*Live!*"
As in, what we're all attempting to do in life
creatively.

Tattoo it on your arm
then maybe you'll understand it better,
and own the meaning
(as he does).

Now back to you…
youth accepted you well,
and with you still.

I remember you sing-dancing once
with poetic words,
making me wonder if I still could?

Your ways somehow keep pushing me
and this dark, ink-filled pen
back to paper.

Now
it tends to write in lighter shades,
with visions amorous and composed.

Always yearning
for those unattainable words,
hoping to convey all that you are,
and all you create in me.

Waiting on 7 a.m.
that's when her show comes on.
And I'm always intrigued to watch.

Gypsy

I can love you,
but I also cannot at the same time.
It's complicated.

These were her words,
expelled under glowing lights
distinct through familiar,
written, then set aflame.

Displaying all of her color
while burning desire,
felt the same.

Lighting up closed minds
with her touch for change,
inviting eyes while arousing sight,
forever making you feel alive.

Holding a spirit
free for the world…

A floating essence for life
always carried through,
inhaled only with privilege,
understood by few.

(Nice to have met you).

Expose Your Motive

Drink coffee out of a wine glass.
Eat pasta with your hands and share it with a friend.
Do something you've never done
then make a big deal about it.
(Reminding yourself that you're still alive).

Compliment rude people throughout your day.
Take photographs with complete strangers,
then make a collage for display.
Connecting stories, from merging lifetimes.
(Graphing all of the marks you've made).

Sketch out pictures of your dreams
in a diary to share, to evoke deep conversation.
Tell someone a secret about yourself
just to see what they'll say.
(Satisfaction through reaction).

Dance in random places with whoever is closest,
and unwilling to be your partner.
Allow all the things that make you nervous into your life,
until they all become a part of you.
(Proving that you can cure a disease).

Expose your motive for different,
inviting stares for a lifetime.
Later becoming their motive for envy
of the freedom you have inside.
(Forever inspiring their lives!).

Sleepwalk With Me

Special
the way you bleed through me,
and call out our tendencies.

You're my scar,
the lioness of my life,
stitching up the thoughts
inside our eyes
to coincide.

Here,
as frequent as the rain
is as often I think of you.

Are we ever going to be in love?

The real way,
when letting go
met our lips for the first time.

So stay here, stay feel,
remember our hearts together
while the world stands still.

Come hide behind my mask
while I stitch your face,
healing you with needles
through threads of my past.

Now you're safe.

Stare

One moment
split
subtracting seconds
one turn
one stare
looking back
our eyes
connecting
just once
saying everything
following smile
following you
walking away
while holding
me in place
silent
still reeling
our film
our scenes
turning feelings
in waiting
future memories
already past
visions of us
replayed in mind
still writing
our script
still making
this life

Worth living.

Inadequate

Stripped
naked with emotion,
now vulnerable to giving in
to your heart.

In these moments,
you try and picture yourself
background to anything
drawing attention away.

As nervousness sets in,
steady hands turn motive:
shaking evidence from obvious trees.

Now foreground
begins painting you in…

Blending no longer,
now you're becoming
an imperfect version
of yourself.

With voiceless words
increasing breath
under each effort spoken,
gasping for air, yet still unaware
all that's coming over you.

Then at this moment,
another landslide of emotion
strips you down.

Until you're completely silenced.
Naked.

(Again).

Smile

Your smile is intuitive
reacting under this charm.
Are you sure you belong here?

(Because it's always night in my skies).

It's only a question
posed for an answer with meaning:
moving words
moving, from you to me.

Words maybe never meant in your world
flowing free of wrong,
but for now just advice…

Pictured through glowing frames
in reeling color.

I have just the chords for such an occasion,
for our souls to dance outside these walls.
So act as if you don't hear questions,
and pretend we both belong.

Phantogram

I Don't Blame You
My Only Friend,
We're Nothing But Trouble.

As Far As I Can See…

You are my Mouthful Of Diamonds,
You Are The Ocean
Washing off my Bloody Palms,
When I'm Small.

Now Let Me Go…

16 Years
All Dried Up,
Don't Move,
Make A Fist,
Fall In Love.

10,000 Claps
Celebrating Nothing,
The Day You Died.

Our Futuristic Casket
Turning Into Stone,
Running From The Cops,
Never Going Home.

Now Turn It Off…

Nightlife,
Bad Dreams,
Black Out Days,
A Dark Tunnel,
With both of our Voices…

Howling At The Moon.

Dance

You spark the tunes
and we'll spark the riot!

Gravity escapes our bodies
with the beat never giving in,
taking over our souls,
setting us in motion…
of forever.

Dub the repetition of sickness,
united we move and believe as one.
Stepping into the light of darkness
where we all create free together,
unafraid.

A relentless force only imagined,
now and forever ours!

Ride

Together as one
we take flight without wings,
riding free from the world
clearing every thought
inside our minds.

In our world
all of our troubles float away,
leaping above new heights
where time turns into miles…
together in stride for all we believe.

Passionate and possessed
we're connected in thought
unlike anything imagined,
reading every step to come
while fearing nothing in our way.

Forever unified
while holding rein to our souls,
endlessly voicing our love
without words.

With over a decade of memories shared
still guiding who we are today,
nothing, or no one
can ever take that away.

About No One

She's a closet redneck
with coat hanger fantasies,
more disappointing
than rubber bristles on a toothbrush.

(French people don't get my humor).

A heavy bottle with a red label
is all she needs to get by.
Bud told me so.

Light would never fly with her,
which is why I can't speak of her lightly.
She's tolerable standing aside
only when used to block the wind
in hard winter.

Her life
is no longer full of water fountains anymore,
to make-up-kiss her way back
to *Great Expectations*.

So guess
what happened the night before?
Then keep guessing.
Therein lies the fun, and my point
of interest.

Getting mud-drunk
is her way of life now,
where it takes her two showers
just to feel honest again.

And honestly
I'm just laughing on the inside,
but I still choose to pay attention
because gutter minds are colorful.

Under The Influence

Under it
they can't see me,
or what this mind can be.

They can't feel all that's right
inside this heart they've wronged.

But they still got me, at nothing,
and at goodbye, before hello.

Invective

On the other side of the fence
across the world
sits a girl...

[Face-to-screen, becoming someone unbecoming].

Guarded with tongue tied,
fingers now fill her void
in versatile ways.

First truth
follows playful aspersion,
to feel humble, unusual,
her reason for being.

Scenarios off-putting to masses
now come alive in mind,
evoking mystery of envy,
foreign most times...

[Translated through word-filled screen].

Immersed in desire
erotic depth escapes reality,
ever pursuing lengths too far
captivating your love-in-like
for her.

Then with unrefined meaning
still seeping through pain,
the same time tomorrow...

[You'll meet her again].

Hook, Line, Sinking

Hearts.
Weakened.
Pounding.
Through glass.
Chests.
Unsteady.
Unsung.
Undone.
Under.
Arrest.

Gravity

When clouds cover light
your ray of life still shines,
through skies I look up to
falling inside me.

With a voice
screaming silence
I'm begging for sound,
just to hear you speak
now taking over me.

In the night
you'll see me falling…
weightless, back to ground.

Always toward you
(My Direction).

Pulling me in
with all that you are,
and everything we feel
still holding back inside.

So catch me, this time.

Rivers

We follow rivers
from our hearts
floating logs
building character
with every scene
drifted past.

Experience
soaking through roots
symbolic with structure
under metaphors
from places
met before.

Always moving
place jumping in mind,
through days felt indisposed
consuming night
still living
forever alive!

Dismantle The Bomb

Laying low
with devils before sunrise:
friends, in between quotations.

Who are they now
but a bomb inside your mind?
Timed to repeat the same implosions,
justifying your own advice.

So just smile and wave
as they crash in sequence,
breathing in their transgression
through gills…

Never drowning you.

Souls Unite

Head below water
familiar sinking in,
so move me
in other ways than by force.

Seduce me
with your soul,
show me everything inside.

(Mine is lost).

Hope to meet yours
so my mind can change,
then faith be restored
in souls again.

Water

Count the times
before you're there.
Lines written, stories told.
(Washed away with water).

Predestined-casket-moments,
our daily life savings.
Earned with time, then shadowed.
(Reflected in water).

Temptations vague
in ways spoken.
Letting emotions peel
at their own pace.
(Healing with water).

Joy filtering regret
scripted, then filed with intent.
Subjected memories,
counted on in time.
(Mixing with water).

Your mind.

The Baddest Dude In The Sky
(For Kyle)

For a while there,
I was lost.

Words wouldn't work.
I had to lose myself to find myself again.

Still here.

Now reality sets in,
you're gone...

An unbreakable force
without a trace,
still always in our hearts
for a time, forever long.

Traced now,
are four perfectly painted faces
half resembling you,
with all you created
and brought out in each smiling one.

Your soul was larger than life,
and the great times we had were countless.

We were all brothers united at different,
and the difference was you,
set apart from the rest.

Always looking up to you,
I saw a life lived the way it should be.

So now I'm going to try and make you proud,
by bringing out the best in everyone
the way you did for me.

From now on,
we'll be together in words.

Subliminally,
I know we'll all hear your laughs,
unheard.

And until that day
our souls again unite,
you'll always be…

The Baddest Dude in the sky.

Ascend

Be the fallen as it may,
it's time to write your chapter as they did.
So search for your source, your guts,
then spill it out in epic fashion!

Let the whole world know you're here!
Choose not just to exist,
but to thrive in the presence of those around you.
Be the one they can't help but follow.

If these trees could talk,
how would they speak of you?
How will they remember you
if you're blending in with the rest?

Jump!
It's inside you.
Rooted.
Just waiting to be composed.

A Year, Zero

I feel as if…
dots resemble years.
Like I've spent my whole life asleep,
now awake.

Pinched by an event,
a wake up call,
calling the talent inside
to come flying out.

Wish the phone would ring every day
with you on the other end,
to reset my mind,
and light that fire to be better
every hour, not every year.

No more waiting…
it's time to change clothes,
and stop wearing the weight
they bring.

Ready now
to show them all!
What real creativity sounds like
through sound.

So you lead, and I'll follow.

Calculated Moves

Throw out your lashes
with ego and directness!
A necessary use for life.

With knives
cutting their verbatims
in halves of truth,
unspoken by you.

Now jump off a building!

Throwing your words
into paper-plane-flights of emotion,
carried with confidence
for the whole world to see!

Stand For Your Worth

Do these words still hold up?
Do these lines still stand up
for all we believe?

That voice inside us both
building higher and higher,
elevating our flooring thoughts
before we jump…

Dying to create free!

If you can't feel these words
written with swords arming hearts,
then take down this mic
if it no longer stands up to you!

Just stab me in the back
with all its lies of sound,
now just waves
crashing unheard.

If you no longer believe
in the message we always stood for,
then scream it now!

Only then could I finally sleep,
knowing these words won't work.

Then we could both
lay this drug…

To rest.

Audacity

Real work never ends
when the sun hides
behind the earth.

In darkness
is when you truly see…
if the ideas you create
are worth the world's belief.

Maybe someday
if you're dedicated through night,
you'll bleed the way I see.

Then with time,
you could create something timeless
that the whole world believes,
or even write words
(way better than these).

Writers Anonymous

When your mind

is too important to see daylight,

your eyes have to adjust.

Lucid

The real dreamer sleeps wide awake
throwing caution aside,
planning fantasies untouched
by human eyes.

Creating every reason for being
with every breath taken in,
becoming enlightened through time,
with experience compared to nothing.

Forever learning
that lies surrounding thoughts
define truth, within.

Bruised flowers now left behind
blossom understanding,
slowly illuminating their way
while others follow.

Cast The Dawn

A day
in advance
a warning
unnoticed
untouched
beginning
from an end
so cast the dawn
because we're all that's left
burning moments
fueling dreams
still lucid
building cathedrals
unstudied
unthought
moving time
gaining momentum
through and through
reckless feelings
filling
empty spaces
inside heart
inside needles
drawing pulse
beating emotions
distant
forgotten...

Then there's the blood.

Lights

Lights out
phones off
silence
reflecting thoughts
off mirrored minds
on call
only for her
now let's pretend
we're bears
so hug me like one
and never let go
until hours
turn months
into winter.

Couch Hunting

Leather was hot at times,
still it was like landing
a twelve-point buck in season
(compared to other material).

It's almost winter now,
time to find your bed-palace,
a real life with someone to hold
(in cuddle weather).

Nocturnal Habits

Hit the station tonight
at two thirty-four in the a.m.
for a coffee, and a car wash.
Nocturnals never sleep.

Probably the reason
why I'm buddies with bats and owls.
We're all old and wise with wicked eyes,
always leading dark paths
using more *sense*...
to guide our flights through life.

An owl
used to be a character on my favorite show,
back when I was tall for being small.
Acting alongside my real best friend
who was a little more grounded,
and carried a name with three E's
just like me.

We both wore heart-shaped faces
sleeveless with emotion,
searching every day
for something we had lost.

While these days it seems
the only thing lost...
is rest.

Nowadays,
all of my nocturnal friends rank high
among costumes worn at night.

So maybe one day
someone will dress like me,
and think it's cool
not to sleep.

Sixth Sense

If sleep were a sixth sense,
maybe I would get some…

I would *see* a place to crash in every moment
always *hearing* darkness calling for me,
forever *tasting* clouds through sound
while *smelling* fuel to ignite my dreams.

Then every time I woke up
I would still *touch* myself,
to get my day going
(on the up and up).

Dig

Buried
to see
under water
dirty
under cover
pushing scenes
clean to clean
this guy's weird
mean for means
glowing thunder
shattered cover
through all it seems
still unclean
this guy
is me.

Deception Of Siren

Line after line,
follows line.

Engulf the fear of now,
of knowing the real,
inside the outside.

Comfort never existed
fashioned in its own lie,
because the more real you feel
the more unreal this gets,
with your mind
never leaving you at ease.

Now and forever,
adapting to what *lies* inside,
rest assured, you don't know me,
you don't know a fucking thing!

Now
lost for words…
Deceiving your siren.

Divided By Fear

This is your life, divided by fear.

So lie, only if you mean it.
Rewrite your life in theme.
Sick twist your own plot.
The future is now
with every next second,
so climax early
resolve, then climax again.

Dance on the backside of rules.
Believe in invisible figures
and name them *doG*.
Talk about touchy subjects.
Touch yourself.
Chill pills do exist,
listen to *Elliot Smith*.

Think in judgment,
speak without.
Resist, just to exist.
Disappoint the masses,
smile at their thoughts of you failing.
Laugh later.

"Nothing has any meaning
except the meaning you give it."
So make something out of nothing,
put faith in koala bears,
and learn to read...

|Between|.

Echo

Loosely triggered for failure
this gun holds no chamber.
(Because you're not there anymore).

There are worse things than death
and you're capable of all of them.
(Destruction at its finest).

Pulling against time
always searching for hurt to blame your wrath.
(Just waiting for the past to show again).

So have a drink to moving on
or don't, and finally do.
(Sustain).

Filtered insomnia
divided by fear of deaf ears.
(Ultimately creates your world).

With an embassy of emotion
indefinitely awaiting your arrival.
(Though cleverly written at time).

Now running out the door, for the door,
forever blind to capability knocking behind.
(The time to move is on).

Face to reflection
(I speak these words).

Traffic

At times,
my mind is full of traffic
(blowing horns).

I wish it were a carpool lane,
free and clear to move
(always in company).

Right Of Way

Stay out of this lane,
our lane.

We fly fast,
and drive that way too.

Faster than *Elmer's*,
used on shoes.

Adhesive,
mending artistic souls
holding true.

We're in this together,
forever moving
faster than you.

Fascination Street

Love reading here,
inside your soul.
Surprised you can sleep in this weather,
I never could.

Anonymous words
hidden for a lifetime,
still shared in mind
from another life's time.

Your heart,
another mirrored reminder
to never stop caring,
until the day it can.

True love waits
for our kind,
the broken souls we are,
never getting older
only getting better with time.

Now years
are just meaningless numbers.
The same way birthdays became
long ago, for people like us.
So happy, that day, to you!
Twenty-five times.

Learning now
as steps uncover realistic truths,
that those past loves were never real,
since they were never shown the right way to.

Each owning *wicked empty smiles,*
never meant for you.

Now it's time,
to tear down walls
motive for disaster…

Because this life is yours to create,
and break free of their ways!

For a path ahead
now dotted with lines,
dividing what's right in all we believe.

As our fascination street for change…

Awaits to be seen.

Drive

Break lights
For miles ahead
Speed up thoughts
For curious minds.

Our roads past
Fuel empty canvas
Revolving scenes
Mirrored on all sides.

Decisions reflected
Written in pavement
Winding dashes
Lining consequence.

Destination nowhere
Delayed by rain
Pouring direction
Now falling familiar.

Silent cloudburst
Under stars of sky
Unveiling pictures
Misting our eyes.

Lighting paths to come
Hands break mistake
Over broken glass
Future dead ends

Now escaped.

Ageless

How many days have passed
between numbers without meaning?

Lighting candles,
spending paper,
buying recognition,
for feelings.

Endlessly testing
the meanings of words,
like ce-le-bra-tion,
and dis-a-ppoint-ment.

Combining letters,
connecting emotion,
words now meaning more
in smaller doses.

Future calendars
begin marking your time,
the dates you own
now different,
with decades behind.

How old am I?

Just another number forgotten,
one more day closer to dying.

(So get busy livin').

October Sky

Where's the art inside you
my dearest friend?

I feel it's hidden
deep within your weathered heart,
just waiting for the right season
to come bursting out!

A clarity
coming with cold,
on a day, not far away…

Her Dream

If this ink dripped on you
would judgment turn without thought?
If I saved your life in the next life,
would you then take the time to listen?

(Unblocked by your fear of what could be).

In this moment, we're already there.
Just waiting for your nightlight to kick,
and push away your fear of the unknown
that darkness brings.

Worried minds
forever evolve dead ends.
Leaving you nearsighted with thought,
still farsighted from what's real.

Open hearts in confidence
hold keys that break down walls.
Leading certain paths for you to create
all that they believe not possible.

(Using everything I know you hold inside).

Window

Just be yourself

be what you will

it's your life

it's your time

you wouldn't be anything at all

without you

and your mind

and your selfish pride sometimes

it gives you strength

and the will

to survive

this is your window

to the world.

Ode To Frost

We never see in ways that lie,
as the real in everyone
tries to hide.

The words to come won't find their way,
they'll just stay inside
to rot away.

Quicksand

Your sinking trails
bring to mind the essence
of reckless abandonment.

My past reflected, now yours.

As blindness consumes you,
being hand-fed lights
drawing skies of direction,
unwanted.

Gasping for air,
while reaching for hands
no longer willing to be submerged
in your lies.

Now
ignorance divides judgment:
the reason, the blame.

As family trees become motive:
your excuse, they decided
once falling…

Now you.

Walk

If I had shoes

that cured wounds,

I would dance on you.

Without words, without hurt,

Without sound...

Don't Now Always

I can still recall
the taste of your tears,
the time I fell falling...
into you.

There we breathed
instinctive in unison,
the smell, the air,
together interconnected
under filtered rays of sun.

Now undone,
as I come,
as you are,
hearts hold on,
and on,
as you like,
as we were,
willful inside.

Now shatter the glass, the *pane*,
my descending windfall from above,
seen through and through
clouds of voiceless whispers,
and rebellion-filled air.

Now tears are wide,
immersed with reason
while sinking through familiar,
narrowed then revised,
while typing through keys.

Forever embedded inside
who we are today,
are my thoughts,
our words...

of DNA.

Conversation

She always carries bad phone service,
and a bad attitude.
(My provider).

I can read her emotion, even via text,
words jumping tower to tower
hitting my screen
(With tears).

Train

As I step on the four train
I begin to recall last night's events,
long stories, filled with confluence and palaces.

She sat at the bar turning hours,
with our bubble of words
escaping the invective
surrounding.

Dressed in devil-antlers,
she was throwing out lines
roping me in.
Lassoed above like a halo,
covering her true agenda within.

Passing another station toward home,
this record spinning thoughts
continues to play in mind.

As she wrote on a napkin her list of ten:
dashed words I had spoken
ringing with sound,
while feelings began to fall
into their right place of wrong.

Clever girl…
carrying a falsified charm
unnoticed until now.
It takes talent
to cover my ears in such ways,
with imagined hands
blocking out the sound of my real life.

Now I'm hearing only her,
and vision her eyes like knives
cutting through to my soul.

Speeding through the night air,
this train passes squares of districts
blocked in cultured grids,
blowing by squares of time
filled with convergence and lights,
guiding me home.

On the other side of town
lies an unfolded square,
once resting below a glass
filled with ammo for her arsenal.
Now reading misguided lyrics
in numbers counting ten.

Soon realized,
the numbers given
were for another train ride home,
and the last bullets poured, fueling her ego,
were the sound of me hanging up
before she had the chance to call.

Lesson learned.

(Can't have 'em all).

Drop Electric

What do you fancy?

I'm drawn to words
(and her).

Interrupting conversations
with only her looks,
while I'm frozen,
absent for sound.

With a class of words
all their own,
holding inside…

No longer coming out.

Crash Palace

Rational ruins plague your fancy
as your world begins to crumble.
Scenarios of exotic tryst
penetrate now harder
in mind.

Is blowing down your palace with words
what it takes to break up silence?

An exertion of feeling never before heard,
holding a sensation like no other
thought left behind.

Now with pleasure only coming
from an endless pit of emotion,
deep in your bones.

Breathing heavier and harder with every thought,
always steering your mind
closer to completion…

Still living with years to come,
before understanding
its resolution.

Assassin

You are definitely
on my hit list…

(of One).

Quick, witty,
and mind-flirtatious…

As I come undone.

Sneaker Pimp

Together we feel as one,
and with that I know
we'll never be alone.

You've had me tied up
in your style from the start,
and the things we shared
were never far apart.

Forever parallel, side by side
in these lives we lead,
together we can conquer anything.

So until the day
our perfect *souls* are gone,
always know
that we'll remain as one.

Losing Touch

Today

I checked the mail

a block away, without shoes,

to feel young again...

Envelopes Are The Devil

Essential documents,
now commonly used
to wipe tobacco off my hands.
(Reminding them what I really think).

Addressing
all that can't be relieved
with incentive to nowhere.
(A monthly waste of trees).

Cutting
at the very tip of my being
while sealing my future's fate.
(A lifetime payback for karma awaits).

No. 2

Me.

Just another *number*.

Penciled into your life.

Too good to hold on to.

Second to none.

Still *erased* away…

We Will Become Ourselves

Still
learning me
while losing you
through blue moons
under stars
and used-to-be's.

Circumventing
places it went wrong
another song
another dream
now this liver
isn't what it used to be
to guide away the pain
the stain of a love
once sane.

So white moon
white out the past
and write a new one
where we'll be safe
a future place
where our hearts
can forever last.

I Know A Place

Never believe in anything
you can never tame,
wishing now
to fall back to silence.

Do these words still own you, or do I?

Set free your mind,
outside glass houses
surrounding your walls,
because you can still catch life
while you fall…

If you're open with arms to achieve.

So lets finish this thing, this life,
with sober minds composed
to break through.

That way I'll remember you,
and you me,
then all we believed…

Will live on.

Controlled Chaos

Deep in, shallow out…

Four equivocal words
spoken before,
reoccur now.

A feeling, one all its own,
unintentionally created,
now creating me.

So spread this fire
impervious to tame,
with viable knowledge
turning cancerous wisdom,
forever circled the same.

Now create to escape
and smile through flames…

Sympathetic only with time,
ticking thoughts of hope
while I reach for faith.

Vanished only hours
before revealing your merciless fate,
then come firing your epic return…

Now triggered, I await.

Under Water

Thank you
for talking out life last night
in the rain of all places,
under this pouring heart.

You are my umbrella,
keeping me from being soaked
in my own thoughts of madness,
the ones holding me back from creating
all they believe not possible.

Those thoughts
keeping me from making the difference I believe in,
as I bleed with every word.

Hoping only to inspire
all of those weathered hearts,
no longer capable of raining emotion.

To become
the same kind of difference in their lives,
that you are now, in mine.

Descend

Emotion
written
is invisible.

Sight need take over
for the actual,
watching as tears fall
from your chest.

Try and understand true meaning,
behind the backs of thoughts
hidden from reason.
Evoking the real, that is love.

Now whispered thoughts
play back and forth between us,
stirring up emotion carried with wind,
endlessly begging us to sin.

Dioxide-filled caution now exhaled
as we breathe in the persuading sky,
mixing our chemicals, our words,
allowing us to be as one.

Perfect now, the time waited,
unveiling trust coming with love.
Ultimately warming the space
once frozen, inside our hearts.

Picture

*I learned to love for the first time
(inside a raincoat).*

Repelling the world, and all its color.

*Because you're even more beautiful
(in black and white).*

Cloudy Days

*With arms we held
diagnosed under love's umbrella,
with the cure
beneath our fingertips.*

*Inside hands
clasped so tight,
under the rain,
forever due to fall.*

*Shattering desire,
our emotions,
no longer hiding
inside our hearts.*

Secrets Automatic

Tell me
you love me
for what we are
in this moment
for all we have
together
above them
never turning
our backs on real
seductive
through silence
making love
inviting whispers
caring words
gasping breath
inside you
under me
beating hearts
in-between.

Inverted

"I can hold my own," can you?

Tom could
back in '86
with pixie sticks
and good radios
playing The Cure
for sounds
perfect volume
notch loud
and me
upside down.

Never Mess With Sunday

*Missed
is the idea of you
every day.*

*As this beat drifts
under melodic tones
delayed.*

*Our way to communicate
forever playing
everything we need to say.*

Never mess with Sunday.

*When the atmosphere breathes
scenes for us to create,
open for interpretation
then painting us in our way.*

Never mess with Sunday.

*Our day...
Put away.*

Bane

Now...
I want to make music
while ripping your heart out
at the same time.

Creating the things
evolving me.

(You are inspiring).

Romeo And Juliet

Two eyes met that day,
as *Placebo* took our stage.
It was like a dreary cold scene
in Berlin years before,
but for our dark souls it was perfect.

[We laughed].

As the wind chilled our minds
our hearts warmed our thoughts,
as two worlds crossed, from two worlds lost.

[The piano and voices rang again].

With your hands felt glowing in mine
blushed inside the scene we set,
together we danced and swayed
caring for nothing but us,
as the world went away.

We were falling…
ignited with passion under weakness.
With so much being said unsaid
understood by no one but our kind,
fueling all these lines
we once wrote together, without words.

The feelings we felt
our eyes could never hide,
and the love we had staring back
most souls still search to find,
for a lifetime.

Lost in thoughts,
we were musing the sight of our lives
still ahead to come.
Hoping to spend the rest of it together,
untouchable as one.

Two eyes met that day,
taking in more love than hearts should bear
while never looking away.

Leaking with emotion now the same,
remembering a day
that was the beginning of the end…

Be it as it may.

Rainbow

*Burn my eyes
with daylight unfamiliar.*

*Speaking in rays
fueling rain, as bows form.*

*Preferred taste together meshed,
forever coloring breath
of our words.*

*So follow me
to the end of our bows.*

*Follow me
'til the end of our love...*

Inception

Now go
but don't stop
loving
the way we were
because I am
forEver-ett
forever yours
so never forget
the idea of us
hiding
in the back of your mind
forever
haunting you inside
those whispers
holding belief
telling you to come back
where your heart wants to be
to a life
once building strength
while sinking into feelings
but you won't
so I'll just keep writing
page fives without i's
imagining us together
until this heart subsides.

We Own The Night

I sit here
thinking of you
whoever you are
reading these lines
understood or not
appreciate the time.

Writing songs is easy
while holding this guitar
it takes courage
to let you inside
these types of pages
into this mind.

Further and further
while surfacing scars
deciding on memories
to choose or fake
reliving the past is hard
just to make you shake.

Hours turning months
time felt the same
daydreams on film
without stars
while insomnia awakes.

Irony plaguing fantasies
places thought escaped
just another way to create
while reliving the pain.

Now I drink sink water
to cleanse my thoughts
and it's within all these things
why we're worlds apart.

Hide The Crowd

I like to be in the wind
because it feels like someone's there,
as shadows sweep behind the past
there's more of it now,
as seconds pass.

A strange attractor pulling back
all while pushing forward,
seal the seems and rip the world,
ever changing the girl.

A thrill once lost still need be fed
as the thought of failing comes home again,
so increase the lie that hides the past,
unveiling that love won't always last.

Commit To Memory

Slowly you feel the feelings change
as the light to guide you
brightens to a close.

Optimism flows deep within
though the track outside
winds to no ones know.

Living seeps out and feeds the air
while an endless whisper
chills your thought.

Then before the sound
of a comatose emergency
the lie to yourself is bought.

Yesterday's Tomorrow

My heart stopped today,
finding out the reasons for whys
when forever came.

Time doesn't exist,
blissfully coinciding higher power,
yet still believed in and felt inside
as we age in change
unseen.

Filtered circles
wander our eyes across the world
then back to here,
grounded with regret
for misplacing our escape route.

We are all burning buildings
with the floors below us fading away,
so buckle up your life
because the time to jump…

Is now!

Parachute The Sky

Pack up the rights
to your life, and go!

Destination: nowhere here.

Uncertain destiny
turning certain path,
with clarity, now justified.

Ill-lighted facade
conceals false fate,
as dark clouds surround
desolate skies.

Absorbed now is the past
pouring down truth,
word by word,
thought filling thought,
whispered then repeated.

Detour
signed familiar,
permits unbecoming desire
unguided.

Now circumvent reason
secret to most:
deep in, shallow out…
still unanswered,
forever allowed.

Now awake,
and never again forget.

Smoke

Smoke filled rings
launch and freeze the air,
rising one by one
provoked by last nights events.

Keeping tempo
with the thoughts in your mind,
a realized habit of guilt
now can't be escaped,
forever beating inside.

Now with silence
floating off your tongue,
it brings past as *present,*
opening future unallowed.

So stand outside and break time
running with the sun's rays,
leading paths filtering out the same,
for all that's at stake.

Fire Escape

I will no longer inhale your judgment
through this filter,
this city.

It's time for this smoke to clear,
and for these legs to tick steps…
leaving here.

We'll meet up again someday
across these bordering lines,
when these unique ideas jump over the horizon,
exploding into accepting skies!

Somewhere ahead holding true to creation
eventually met before long,
where this mind can be free at its best,
in a place where they believe…

And I belong.

Today

What is today?
I am today, as are you,
and we both hold within us
the emotion for change.

Today we begin...
our journey without courts,
without lanes, roads, or streets,
only avenues, our avenues,
leading us where we both belong.

Coyote Blood made this day,
paving direction for tomorrow's drug.

Movement for new beginnings
that have no ending.

Together *We Are*...
the reasons behind dotted lines
leading paths, defining their lives.

This day is real, one all its own.
Though brought up different,
still brought together.

Blood for blood, We're the Drug.

4:13

*Slowly
paint me the way you see.*

*With saint-like shadows
underneath.*

*Or in the light
you truly believe.*

*Your last chance
to uncover the seams...*

Begin

Sharing time
through night,
painting moving pictures
of our souls drifting away.

Can this be us someday?

As we touch
face to fingertips,
feeling one another
endless with emotion,
hand in hand
now holding each other's lives.

Drawing hearts
on each other's chests
with hands vibrant in color,
open and free
with outstretched arms,
unafraid to feel the end
together.

The first time our eyes met
was the time life truly began,
following years of perception
needed to realize,
that these eyes were made
to see only you.

*Now you know what I always meant
when I said I loved you...
(As friends).*

Duck, You Suckers

Thanks
for reading this,
knowing it's probably eating
into your writing time.

Maybe you felt inspired
somewhere along the *werds?*

Maybe you found a new way
to speak some of your lines unheard?

Four steps ahead,
the way our minds think,
for a new story
you may already have in yours now,
just maybe.

As nontraditional ideas
slowly begin to feel traditional,
back and forth through messages
with our words,
becoming our tradition.

Words
no longer in-boxed unheard,
instead now shared as turning works of art:
swift-movement-through-pages
forever holding our message…

To the world.

Keep One Eye Open

What ever happened to the art inside people?
I feel it's been silenced
somewhere deep.

Lower than heart, under ribs,
jail bars holding the weak.

Though temporary with warning
the alarm is now set for you to speak,
rising words screaming morning,
your time to wake them up to believe!

Now I spend my days
admiring the unforgettable people:
all of those artists that have made a mark on me.

So if you believe,
stand up and speak free!

About me.
About this movement.
For us.
For art, in all its forms.
Felt deep!

Start spreading your own ideas of creation,
and never again…

Be put to sleep!

When The World Ends

When the world ends
all the knives will be washed away,
so no taking the easy route,
as we're in this together.

Now uncover the filter to your words,
speak all the lines you've never said
to all those people unwilling to hear.

Document your life's diary
by seeping it into someone else's mind,
so when all the pages written are lost
our calendars will live on
inside one another.

Leaving no regrets behind
we can all wear smiles on our souls,
for transfer attire.

Then on that day
when we finally meet again,
we can all high-five ourselves
in the clouds.

Built For Forever

*This is what it will read next to our names
when we're long gone,
buried under the streets...*

Next to our script
engraved in cement,
our last words, a final form of ink
everlasting, for the world to perceive.

To ponder
over all we've done,
inspiring eyes for a lifetime...

Eternally challenging everything
their lost souls aspire to be,
because their hands could never paint
the canvas of words we've seen.

We're The Drug

With water now under the bridge,
we're baring skin to sound.

We're the drug
feeding off of night,
preying on thoughts unheard
to be spoken out loud.

Unfiltered in disregard,
consequence no longer exists.

We're the drug
vaulted above the rest,
painting ceilings with thoughts,
building cathedrals with words.

Become the voice
allowing us in,
our favorite brush
shading color for movement.

Our timeless vision
time be let out,
swaying emotions never before felt,
tucked away until now.

We're the drug
lawless in mind,
with purpose we rise,
violating all that's said be normal
one line at a time.

An understanding within,
misunderstood by them.

We're the drug undenied,
the anecdote for change.
Art gets unburied here.
The time is now!

THE ~~END~~.

BEGINNING...

Musical Inspirations

Phantogram
The Knife
Metric
Little Dragon
Placebo
Chvrches
Civil Twilight
If These Trees Could Talk
Deas Vail
Elliott Smith
Deftones
Cults
Radiohead
Death Cab For Cutie
Keaton Henson
Banks
The Cure
Nine Inch Nails
Bob Marley
Yppah
Silversun Pickups
Lana Del Rey
Jimmy Eat World
Lykke Li
Dave Matthews Band
The Myriad
Uh Huh Her
Garbage
Thrice
Band Of Horses
Lorde
Emma Louise
Incubus
Damien Rice
Jason Mraz
Kings Of Leon
Smashing Pumpkins
Stone Temple Pilots
Pearl Jam

Made in the USA
Columbia, SC
16 June 2019